INSIDE!
YOUR AWESOME MATCH ANNUAL 2015!

OI! BIG HEAD 18

TRANSFER EXCLUSIVE 8

TOP 50 BIGGEST TRANSFERS 40

SNAPPED 38 & 62

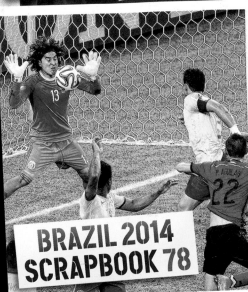

BRAZIL 2014 SCRAPBOOK 78

KINGS OF THE WORLD! NO.4 CRISTIANO RONALDO

RONALDO KOTW 68

SUBSCRIBE TO MATCH – TURN TO PAGE 92 FOR MORE INFO!

2015?
BRING IT ON!

LIVERPOOL and ex-ENGLAND captain STEVEN GERRARD tells MATCH why he thinks 2015 will blow our socks off!

STEVIE ON...

2015 BUZZ!

"The success Liverpool had in the Premier League in 2013-14 was a big step forward for us as a group of players. Looking forward to 2015, I think the squad has become stronger under a great manager and we will go from strength to strength!"

STEVIE ON...

RISING STARS!

"I've been lucky enough to see Raheem Sterling, Jordan Henderson and Jon Flanagan all establish themselves in the Liverpool team, and I think they have the skill and temperament to be world-class players. Beyond Liverpool, Alex Oxlade-Chamberlain, Ross Barkley and Calum Chambers all demonstrate England is in pretty good shape!"

2015 FACT!
Stevie will enter his 18th year as a Liverpool first-team player in 2015! Now that's experience!

0

Arsenal are the only team in Premier League history to go the whole season unbeaten! They finished 2003-04 with 26 wins, 12 draws and no defeats!

THIS KIT TOTALLY SUCKS!

632

Man. United legend Ryan Giggs has played 632 Prem games – that's more than any other player! Frank Lampard and Gareth Barry are the only current stars in the Premier League's top five all-time appearance list!

1

Derby only won one Prem game in 2007-08! They bagged just 11 points and finished with a -69 goal difference, too! All three are painful Prem records!

DID YOU KNOW?

Berlin's Olympic Stadium will host the 2015 Champo League Final! It also staged the 2006 World Cup Final!

Moneybags UNITED!

I'M GETTING GOLD-PLATED F50S!

Adidas have signed a £750 million deal with Man. United to make their kits for the next ten years, starting from 2015! Louis van Gaal's transfer budget will be off the charts!

DORTMUND STAR MARCO REUS...
THE WORLD'S MOST WANTED!

> IT'S TIME TO CELEBRATE AGAIN!

NET-BUSTER!

'Rolls Reus' bagged 16 Bundesliga goals in just 26 starts last season! He's got the movement of an experienced striker in the 18-yard box, packs a rocket shot from distance and has ice-cool finishing skills! He can do it all!

> REUS IS LETHAL, JA?

SPEED DEMON!

The Borussia Dortmund and Germany forward is one of the quickest stars in world footy and skins defenders like a turbo-charged cheetah! Real Madrid couldn't handle his pace when he hit a Champo League double past them last season!

ARSENAL'S HOPPING HERO!

Arsenal's Alexis Sanchez once found a rabbit on a road and took it home, because loads of wild boar were in the area!

2014 FIFA World Cup™ Champions

8

Germany reached their eighth World Cup final last summer, which is a new record

WHO WANTS HIM?

ASSIST MACHINE!

Reus isn't just a speedy goal king – he loves setting up his team-mates for scoring chances, too! He grabbed nine awesome Bundesliga assists in 2012-13 and a massive 13 last season! Just call him, 'Mr. Assists!'

MASSIVE BARGAIN!

We've heard Reus has a special release clause in his contract, which lets him leave Dortmund in 2015 for just £28 million!

£28m

COPA AMERICA STAT ATTACK!

South America's version of the European Championships takes place this summer!

7
Chile will host the tournament for the seventh time in 2015! Arturo Vidal and Alexis Sanchez will want to rip it up!

15
Uruguay have won the Copa America a record 15 times, including the last tournament in 2011!

12
Jamaica and Mexico will join the ten South American countries to make up the 12-team tournament!

4
Luis Suarez scored four goals in the 2011 event and was named Player Of The Tournament. Legend!

Sergio's Biscuits!

Hobnobs...
with Sergio Busquets!

THEY ARE LEO'S FAVES!

SUPER SCOTT!

Scotland warrior Scott Brown is the most expensive star to move between Scottish clubs! He joined Celtic from Hibernian for £4.4 million back in 2007!

ROSS BARKLEY!

+ FOUR MORE REASONS WHY 2015 IS GOING TO BLOW YOUR MIND!

WICKED WONDERKID!
Ross Barkley should get even better for Everton and England in 2015! His power, dribbling and long shots destroy teams!

REAL ROCK!
Real Madrid are aiming to become the first team in history to win back-to-back Champions League trophies. We can't wait to see their attacking stars going all out for glory!

MEGA-TIGHT TITLE RACE!
Last season's Premier League title race blew our eyeballs out, but we reckon it'll be even crazier in 2015! Absolutely anyone can win it!

MESSI & RON ON THE MOVE?
The football world will go transfer crazy again next summer! Is Lionel Messi finally coming to the Premier League? Will Cristiano Ronaldo head back to Man. United?

RED-HOT RAHEEM!
Raheem Sterling has the talent to become one of the top ten stars in world footy in 2015! The Liverpool star gives defenders nightmares with his electric pace!

PAGE 56

PAGE 30

PAGE 86

KINGS OF THE WORLD!

Everything you need to know about the world's greatest players!

PAGE 12

LUIS SUAREZ

ARJEN ROBBEN

LIONEL MESSI

GARETH BALE

CRISTIANO RONALDO

PAGE 68

KINGS OF THE WORLD!

NO.1 GARE

GOAL KING!

Bale netted 42 Premier League goals in six seasons, but exactly half of them came in 2012-13!

FACE OF FIFA!

The Real ace has huge

DOUBLE DELIGHT!

Bale's only the third player ever – after Andy Gray and Cristiano Ronaldo - to win both the PFA Player and Young Player Of The Year awards in the same season!

BALE'S ROYAL PATH!

1989
A king is born!

1998
He's scouted at the PlayStation Schools' Cup in Newport!

1998
Signs up to train with Southampton's academy!

2006
Makes his Saints debut in 2-0 win over Millwall!

TH BALE

SCHOOL DAYS!
He went to Whitchurch High School in Cardiff and played football with current Wales rugby captain Sam Warburton!

WAG WATCH!
He lives in Madrid with his girlfriend Emma Rhys-Jones and they have a daughter together called Alba Violet!

SOCIAL MEDIA SUPERSTAR!
The Welsh wizard has nearly 20 million likes on Facebook, almost five million followers on Twitter and over two million Instagram fans!

FOOTY IDOL!
Man. United and Wales legend Ryan Giggs was Bale's hero when he was growing up!

SPEED MACHINE!
Bale was awesome at athletics when he was younger and once ran 100 metres in 11.4 seconds!

2006
Becomes Wales' youngest ever player, then goalscorer!

2007
Joins the Prem after a £7 million move to Tottenham!

2009
Suffers a mad 24-match winless run for Spurs!

2010
Hits an epic Champo League hat-trick past Inter Milan!

2013
Wins PFA Player Of The Year award!

2013
Joins Real Madrid for a world record £85.3 million!

2014
Stars as Real Madrid win the Champions League!

KING OF SKILLS!

MEGA POWER!

Nobody ever talks about Bale's strength, but the way he shrugged off Barça defender Marc Bartra for his famous goal in the Copa del Rey final last season was crazy! He obviously hit the gym hard last summer too, because he's beefed up loads recently!

SCORE: 90/100

SIZZLING SPEED!

Bale was clocked sprinting at almost 25mph against Villarreal last season, which is just two mph slower than Usain Bolt's speed when he broke the 100 metre world record! That's how fast the Welsh wizard can burn you up!

SCORE: 98/100

DEADLY DRIBBLING!

The Wales legend used to be all about pace and power, but he's picked up some lethal dribbling skills! His main party trick is to knock the ball 20 metres past his opponent, then run around him and receive his own pass!

SCORE: 95/100

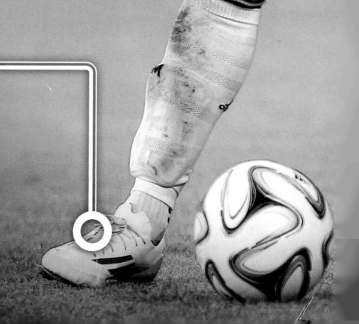

EXPERT FINISHER!

It's crazy to think Bale started his career as a left-back, because he's now one of the planet's deadliest finishers! He netted 21 Prem goals in 2012-13, including 16 with his left foot, then scored 22 times in his debut season for Real Madrid!

SCORE: 91/100

DEAD-BALL DEMON!

Bale's left foot is a lethal weapon, and he uses it to crash home unstoppable free-kicks! He has different techniques too! Sometimes he smashes through the ball with his laces, but he can also use his instep to get mind-boggling swerve!

SCORE: 92/100

WIN!

A PAIR OF ADIDAS INSTINCT BOOTS

Signed by Juan Mata!

Thanks to our mates at Adidas, we're giving away a pair of the awesome Instinct Predators to one lucky MATCH reader! And to make this prize even better, they'll be signed by Man. United and Spain midfielder Juan Mata!

HERE'S HOW TO ENTER!

CLOSING DATE: January 31

THE LIGHTNING SQUAD

Speed Machine!

There are loads of rapid heroes in the Premier League, but Theo Walcott might be the quickest of the bunch! The Arsenal speedster leaves his marker choking on dust once he accelerates past them and burns away!

Theo's Stats!

Five-yard bursts	92
Weaving runs	94
Long sprints	97
Dribbling control	87
Top speed	99

He should be called...

The Ferrari!

WALCOTT

ARSENAL

BIG H

MATCH checks out w
stars might get up

Joe
THE BA

The Cit
can't ge
around

I WAN
SEE MY
IN IT

Leo Messi..
@ THE CAR WASH!

Even the
world's best
player needs
a sparkling car!

BIG MATCH! QUIZ

PREMIER LEAGUE SPECIAL

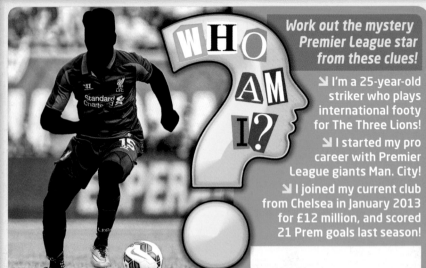

WHO AM I?

Work out the mystery Premier League star from these clues!

↘ I'm a 25-year-old striker who plays international footy for The Three Lions!

↘ I started my pro career with Premier League giants Man. City!

↘ I joined my current club from Chelsea in January 2013 for £12 million, and scored 21 Prem goals last season!

---

5 QUESTIONS ON...

ALEXIS SANCHEZ

Arsenal

1 How much did The Gunners sign Alexis for - £23 million, £33 million or £43 million?

2 Arsenal signed the red-hot forward from Barcelona, but which club did Barça sign him from – Juventus, Napoli or Udinese?

3 How many goals did the Chile megastar score at Brazil 2014 – two, three or four?

4 What shirt number does he wear for the north London giants - No.7, No.17 or No.27?

5 True or False? The lightning-quick forward is the first ever Chilean to play for Arsenal!

FLIPPED!

Which Prem manager has had his face messed up in this bonkers pic?

SOCCER SCRABBLE

Unscramble these letters to work out an awesome goal machine's name!

E₁ E₁ V₄ R₁ N₁ N₁ A₁ C₃ L₁ I₁ E₁ N₁

Premier League BRAIN-BUSTER!

How much do you know about the Prem?

1. Which three teams were promoted to the Premier League in 2013-14?

2. Man. City won the title by how many points last season?

3. In which year did the Premier League begin – 1992, 1994 or 1996?

4. Which team play their home games at the Liberty Stadium?

5. What position did Chelsea finish in the table last season?

6. Which Premier League club's stadium has the biggest capacity?

7. How many times have Arsenal won the Prem title?

8. Which team scored the most goals in the 2013-14 season?

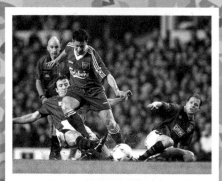

9. How many teams have played in every single Premier League season – five, six or seven?

10. Which £59.7 million megastar is the Prem's record buy?

1 ....
2 ....
3 ....
4 ....
5 ....
6 ....
7 ....
8 ....
9 ....
10 ....

ANSWERS ON PAGE 91

THE NEXT

PATRICK ROBERTS
Fulham & England

MINI MESSI!

Patrick's pace and dribbling skills put him up there with the best teenage wingers in the world! His fearless running in tight areas and confidence to pull off a trick to escape his marker mean the nickname 'Mini Messi' is exactly right!

LONG-SHOT LEGEND!

As well as being a great creator of goals, Roberts knows how to score them too! He loves cutting in off the right wing and whipping shots into the far corner of the net, and he's a free-kick expert from 25 yards!

EARLY FAME!

Patrick first caught the eye when he played for Fulham in a Premier League Futsal tournament back in 2012! Fellow England Under-17 team-mates Ryan Ledson and Isaiah Brown starred as well!

MEGA FACTPACK!

Name: Patrick Roberts
Age: 17
Position: Right winger/Forward
Club: Fulham
Country: England
Boots: Adidas F50 adizero
Top Skill: Dribbling around defenders!

BIG THING!

MATCH reveals the young player who's set to become a megastar in 2015!

PRO DEAL!

Roberts signed his first professional contract in February 2014! The deal tied The Cottagers' wonderkid to the club until the summer of 2016, but that hasn't stopped some of the biggest teams in Europe from sending out spies to watch him!

YOUNG LIONS SUCCESS!

Patrick's biggest achievement so far came when he won the European Under-17 Championships in 2014! He was awesome, bagged three goals and was even named in the Team Of The Tournament!

PATRICK'S BIG STATS!

DRIBBLING		9
PACE		9
LONG SHOTS		8
PASSING		8
FOOTY BRAIN		8
CROSSING		7

HUGE PRAISE!

Felix Magath named Roberts in Fulham's first-team squad for the home game against Newcastle on March 15, 2014! In the post-match interview, he described Patrick as an 'extraordinary talent'!

YOUTH CUP FINALIST!

Pat starred and scored as Fulham narrowly lost 7-6 to west London rivals Chelsea in the two-legged FA Youth Cup final last year!

ENGLAND STAR!

The wicked Fulham wonderkid has played for England's Under-16 and Under-17 teams, and we reckon he'll become a key member of the Under-21s in 2015!

TURN OVER TO SEE MORE STARS WHO'LL ROCK 2015!

NEW WORLD B

ADAMA TRAORE

Winger ★ 18 years old
Barcelona ★ Spain

Barça's latest wonderkid has two of the fastest feet in footy, and he uses them to tie defenders in knots! His rapid acceleration, ability to roll out tricks at speed and pick out lethal crosses mean he'll be starring at the Nou Camp alongside Messi and Suarez in 2015!

Adama's Stats!

DRIBBLING		8
PACE		9
CROSSING		9
LONG SHOTS		7
STRENGTH		9

RYAN GAULD

Midfielder ★ 18 years old
Sporting Lisbon ★ Scotland

Sporting signed 'Baby Messi' from Dundee United in July and immediately slapped a £48 million buy-out clause on his head! He'll need time to settle in to Portuguese footy, but his awesome technique, amazing balance and clever feet mean he'll become a superstar!

Ryan's Stats!

PASSING		8
LONG SHOTS		8
FOOTY BRAIN		9
PACE		9
TRICKS		8

MEMPHIS DEPAY

Winger ★ 20 years old
PSV Eindhoven ★ Holland

Magic Memphis has been floating around the Eredivisie with PSV for almost three years, but it's in 2015 that he'll take his game to the next level! The Dutch winger's driving runs, crazy dipping long shots and jaw-dropping tricks are world-class!

Memphis' Stats!

DRIBBLING		8
PACE		9
CROSSING		7
LONG SHOTS		8
STRENGTH		8

EATERS 2015

SIMONE SCUFFET

...alkeeper ★ 18 years old
Udinese ★ Italy

...ne sounds like the last thing you
...do when you're kicking a footy,
...18-year-old is ripping up Serie A
...w! He's caught the eye of Italian
...perts with a string of rock-solid
...s for Udinese, and is tipped to
...own the No.1 shirt in 2015!

Simone's Stats!

...PPING		9
...NG		8
...TH		8
...NT		7
		8

ADNAN JANUZAJ

Winger ★ 19 years old
Man. United ★ Belgium

United's Belgian flyer showed he could
terrify Prem defences with his dribbling
and acceleration in 2014, but 2015 will
be the year he really goes big-time! The
19-year-old's unique top-spin crosses,
rapid pace, slick technique and missiled
deliveries are a deadly combination!

Adnan's Stats!

DRIBBLING		9
PACE		8
CROSSING		9
LONG SHOTS		8
STRENGTH		6

THESE KIDS AREN'T BAD EITHER!

GEDION ZELALEM
MIDFIELDER
Arsenal &
Germany

RYAN LEDSON
MIDFIELDER
Everton &
England

DAVIE SELKE
STRIKER
Werder Bremen
& Germany

ADRIEN RABIOT
MIDFIELDER
PSG &
France

ADAM ARMSTRONG
STRIKER
Newcastle
& England

Stats correct up to November 1, 2014.

Fit 2...
...grid!

Azpilicu...
Barzagli...
Diaz Ma...
Gotze Ba...
Guzan As...
Hazard C...
Januzaj M...
Lavezzi P...
Mahrez L...
Mandzuk...

ZABALETA
PSG

ROBBEN

HANS' THE MAN!
Arjen's dad Hans works as his agent and footy adviser! He sorts out all of his big-money deals and hardly ever misses a game at the Allianz Arena!

MASSIVE WHEELS!
We've spotted the Dutch master in three different cars in the last year, but the one he drives most often is a bright white, top-of-the-range Audi Q7!

MEGA MONEY!
Robben signed a new contract with German champs Bayern Munich last March worth around £160,000 a week! He has monster deals with Adidas and Audi too!

BRAZILIAN HERO!
The wing wizard was a huge fan of legendary Barcelona and PSV striker Romario when he was growing up! The Brazil goal machine was awesome at the 1994 World Cup!

2005
Stars as The Blues win their first league title for 50 years!

2004
Goes big-time when he joins Chelsea for £12.1 million!

2007
Joins Real Madrid and wins La Liga in first season!

2009
He's sold to Bayern Munich for a massive £22 million!

2010
Wins the double and Bundesliga Player Of The Year award!

2013
Wins Champions League after a MOTM display!

2014
One of the stars of Brazil 2014 as Holland finish third!

KING OF SKILLS!

SCARY SPEED!

The Dutch bullet was recorded running a mind-blowing 23mph in Brazil last summer, which makes him the fastest World Cup footballer of all time! His ability to hit top speed from a slow jog, with or without the ball, will make your eyeballs spin!

SCORE: 98/100

MAD BALANCE!

If you pause your TV when Robben's running past a defender, you'll see just how far he leans to the left and right... it's crazy! The Bayern flyer's over ten centimetres taller than Leo Messi, but his balance and ability to weave in and out at impossible angles is every bit as good!

SCORE: 96/100

AMAZING VISION!

Every footy fan knows about Robben's dribbling skills, but his talent for spotting an unseen pass is less well known. The Dutch destroyer regularly changes the play with a perfect cross-field pass, or splits a defence wide open with a 'no look' through ball!

SCORE: 92/100

UNREADABLE SHAPE!

Every defender in world footy knows Robben wants to cut inside on his left foot and strike at goal when he gets them one-on-one! But the rapid speed he moves the ball, and the way he draws in his shoulders to disguise his plan, mean it's almost impossible stopping him from doing what he wants!

SCORE: 93/100

LEFT-FOOT HAMMER!

There aren't many better finishers right now than Bayern's No.10! He takes his shots really early, leaving keepers no time to react to his flicked or side-foot finishes. When serious power is needed to find the net from long range, his left foot always delivers too!

SCORE: 94/100

MATCH

BIG MATCH! QUIZ

CHAMPIONS LEAGUE SPECIAL

FOOTY AT THE FILMS!

Which La Liga megastar has taken the place of Alex in Madagascar?

BOGUS BADGE!

1925

Which class club's badge has been jumbled up?

ODD ONE OUT!

Basel   Schalke   Liverpool   Monaco

AC Milan

SCP SPORTING PORTUGAL

Sporting Lisbon

Which of these teams isn't playing in this season's competition?

BACK TO THE FUTURE

Which Liverpool new boy has gone back in time to lift the trophy in 2005?

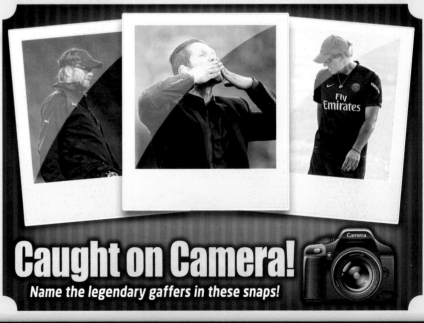

Caught on Camera!

Name the legendary gaffers in these snaps!

5 QUESTIONS ON...
THE CHAMPIONS LEAGUE

1 Which European superclub has won the Champions League a record ten times - AC Milan, Barcelona or Real Madrid?

2 Which awesome German stadium will host this season's CL final - Munich's Allianz Arena, Berlin's Olympic Stadium or Dortmund's Signal Iduna Park?

3 How many English teams have won the famous trophy since the competition began back in 1955 - three, four or five?

4 At the start of 2014-15, who was the Champions League's all-time top scorer - Messi, Raul, Shevchenko or Del Piero?

5 Which awesome sports brand designs the Champions League football - Nike, Adidas, Under Armour, Warrior or Puma?

2014

2012

GUESS THE WINNERS!
Which teams won the Champo League trophy in these years?

2010

2008

AZERBAIJAN LAND OF FIRE
1. *atletico*

T
2. ?

Jeep
3. *new*

🔍 SPOT THE SPONSOR!
Which 2014-15 CL teams have these sponsors on their shirts?

SAMSUNG
4. *chelsea*

ÆGON
5. ?

QATAR AIRWAYS
6. *Barca*

BONKERS FANS!

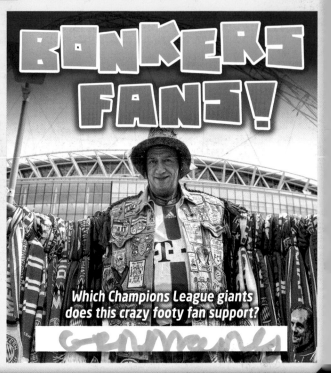

Which Champions League giants does this crazy footy fan support?
germany

ANSWERS ON PAGE 91

Speed Machine!

The Spurs winger has been one of the fastest players on the planet for almost ten years, and he's showing no sign of slowing down! His close control and ability to weave past defenders at speed is legendary!

Aaron's Stats!

Five-yard bursts	93
Weaving runs	92
Long sprints	85
Dribbling control	94
Top speed	96

He should be called...

The Cheetah!

AARON LENNON
TOTTENHAM

CROSSWORD CRUNCH!

Use the clues to fill in MATCH's mega footy crossword!

ACROSS

2. Famous Italian city that Lazio and Roma call home! (4)

5. Awesome Championship team known as The Canaries! (7)

7. Man. United's power-packed car shirt sponsor! (9)

12. Real Madrid legend who top scored in the Champions League last season! (9,7)

14. Powerful Belgium goal king, Christian _ _ _ _ _ _ _! (7)

16. Chelsea and Spain midfielder, Cesc _ _ _ _ _ _ _ _! (8)

18. Spanish club who won the 2013-14 Europa League! (7)

19. First name shared by Atletico Madrid gaffer Simeone and new Chelsea striker Costa! (5)

20. The 2014 World Cup Final was played in this stadium! (8)

21. Sports brand who designed Arsenal's kit this season and make the evoSPEED boot! (4)

22. Nickname of Prem new boys Burnley, The _ _ _ _ _ _ _! (7)

23. Man. United signed midfield master Ander Herrera from this quality La Liga team! (8,6)

DOWN

1. Euro 2016 hosts! (6)

3. Chelsea gaffer Jose Mourinho was born in this country! (8)

4. Last season's Championship play-off winners! (3)

6. The club who lost last season's FA Cup final against Arsenal! (4)

8. Wolfsburg, Paderborn, Freiburg and Eintracht Frankfurt play in this awesome league! (10)

9. Colombia sensation who hit six goals at the 2014 World Cup to win the Golden Boot! (5,9)

10. Man. City's opponents on the final day of the Prem season! (11)

11. World Cup quarter-finalists and England's final Group D opponents at Brazil 2014! (5,4)

13. London-based Championship team who play at The Den! (8)

14. Senegal and Besiktas goal machine, Demba _ _! (2)

15. Solid Holland and Aston Villa centre-back, Ron _ _ _ _ _! (5)

17. Sports brand who make the epic F50 and Predator boots! (6)

21. Peterborough's nickname and David Beckham's wife! (4)

ANSWERS ON PAGE 91

SNAPPED!
BEST OF 2014! PART ONE

When toilet roll attacks!

Scissor guff!

Bony's pumping technique is mad!

Welbeck's got tekkers!

Naismith's in trouble!

Who nicked the ref's choccy bar?

Worst Hide And Seek ever!

TOP 50
BIGGEST TRANSFERS
OF ALL TIME!

MATCH counts down the biggest buys in football history from 50-1!

50 Willian

£30 million

Anzhi to Chelsea

August 2013

Willian pulled off one of the great transfer U-turns in 2013! The skilful winger was minutes away from signing for Spurs, only for Chelsea to make a last-minute move and snatch the Brazilian trickster from under the north London club's nose!

49 Fernandinho

UKRAINIAN LEAGUE'S RECORD SALE!

£30 million

Shakhtar Donetsk to Man. City

June 2013

Fernandinho was so desperate to sign for City – and end his eight-year stay in Ukraine – that he told Shakhtar they could keep £4 million of his wages if it got the deal done! The Brazilian went on to become City's first-choice defensive midfielder in 2013-14!

47 Andriy Shevchenko

MOST EXPENSIVE UKRAINIAN OF ALL TIME!

£30 million
AC Milan to Chelsea
June 2006

The Blues had been linked with a world-record breaking bid for AC Milan goal machine Shevchenko in 2005. But it wasn't until a year later that 'Shevagol' finally joined the Stamford Bridge club – and for nearly £20 million less than the year before!

£30 million
Inter Milan to Real Madrid
August 2002

Big Ron battled back to fitness in the 2001-02 season to bag his third World Player Of The Year award. He was strong, quick and could score goals most strikers would only dream of, and that was enough to convince Real they had to sign him!

45 Rio Ferdinand

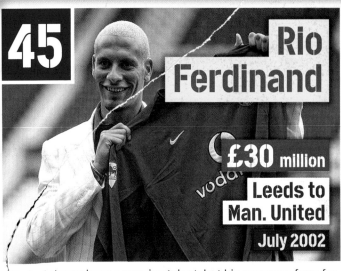

£30 million
Leeds to Man. United
July 2002

Rio had always been a massive talent, but his awesome form for Leeds in 2001 convinced Sir Alex Ferguson to make him the rock at the heart of Man. United's defence! His mix of pace, power and ice-cool timing made him one of the best defenders in the world!

44 Rui Costa

AC MILAN'S ALL-TIME RECORD SIGNING!

£30 million

Fiorentina to AC Milan

July 2001

Fiorentina were having money troubles in 2001, so when AC Milan offered £30 million for their star midfielder they couldn't say no. The Portugal playmaker struggled to find his best form in Milan, but still won a Champions League and Serie A title with the club!

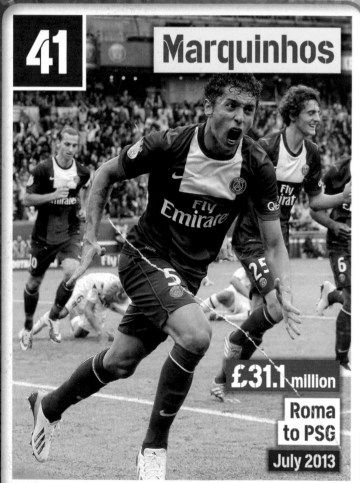

41 Marquinhos

£31.1 million

Roma to PSG

July 2013

Mega-rich PSG showed how serious they were about taking over as Europe's biggest club by burning £31.1 million on Marquinhos! The speedy Brazilian has only started a handful of games since then, but at just 20 years old he's only going to get better!

40 Mario Gotze

£31.5 million

B. Dortmund to Bayern Munich

July 2013

Gotze went from Borussia hero to zero when he announced plans to join rivals Bayern before Dortmund's massive Champions League semi-final first leg against Real Madrid. Bayern went on to beat Dortmund in the final, with Mario watching from the stands!

38 Diego Costa

£32 million

Atletico Madrid to Chelsea

July 2014

Costa's career was going nowhere in 2011, but [...] with Rayo Vallecano in 2012 and 27 goals in Atle[tico's] title-winning campaign has turned him into the comple[te] Mourinho believes he can become Chelsea's new Didier D[rogba]

37 Eden Hazard

£32 million

Lille to Chelsea

June 2012

Hazard had proved he was easily the best player in Ligue 1 with two seasons of lightning-fast, goal-packed footy, so he was ready for a new challenge! Chelsea moved first ahead of loads of other big clubs to match Lille's monster valuation, and Eden was a Blue!

36 Christian Vieri

20TH CENTURY RECORD!

£32 million

Lazio to Inter Milan

June 1999

The powerhouse striker played for 13 clubs during his career, but it was his move from Lazio to Inter Milan that shot him into super stardom! The £32 million fee was a world record at the time and he paid Inter back with strength, accuracy and loads of goals!

35 Robinho

£32.5 million

Real Madrid to Man. City

September 2008

The arrival of Robinho at the Etihad Stadium moved Man. City from being big dreamers to massive players in the footy world! Although the Brazil trickster struggled to adapt to the power of the English game, his boost to City's status was enormous!

34 Gianluigi Buffon

MOST EXPENSIVE KEEPER OF ALL TIME!

£32.6 million
Parma to Juventus
July 2001

Juve more than doubled the £15.7 million Lazio paid Inter Milan for Angelo Peruzzi in 2000 to make Buffon the most expensive keeper ever! The Italy No.1's world-class handling means he'll go down in history as one of the greatest stoppers of all time!

32 Luka Modric

£33 million
Tottenham to Real Madrid
August 2012

Modric grew into a world-class playmaker during his spell at Spurs, but he became frustrated at their failure to challenge for the title. Chelsea had a £40 million bid for him turned down in the summer of 2011, before Spurs decided to sell to Real a year later!

31 Asier Illarramendi

£34 million
Real Sociedad to Real Madrid
July 2013

Every footy fan knows the one thing Real Madrid love doing is spending huge amounts of money on new players, so nobody was surprised when Carlo Ancelotti paid Real Sociedad £34 million for one of the fastest midfield brains and best tacklers in La Liga!

30 Axel Witsel

£34 million
Benfica to Zenit St. Petersburg
September 2012

Manager Luciano Spalletti was handed a sackload of cash to keep Zenit above the Moscow clubs in 2012-13, and he used it to buy one of the most complete midfielders in Europe! Witsel smashes into tackles, runs his socks off and plays killer passes all day long!

29
Javi Martinez

THE BUNDESLIGA'S RECORD SIGNING!

£34 million

Athletic Bilbao to Bayern Munich

August 2012

Bayern planned to change to a clever 4-2-3-1, and ball-playing defensive midfielder Martinez was targeted as the man to make that happen. The German giants matched his £34 million release clause and went on to win the treble in his first season at the club!

28
Cesc Fabregas

£34 million

Arsenal to Barcelona

August 2011

Cesc started his career at Barça, but left the Nou Camp aged 16 for first-team footy with Arsenal. He turned into one of the Prem's best attacking midfielders, and after being dressed in a Barça shirt while on Spain duty it was obvious he was coming home!

27
Javier Pastore

£34 million

Palermo to PSG

August 2011

Pastore joined Palermo as a 20-year-old and quickly proved he could mix it with the best stars in Serie A! Two years and a lot of slick passes later, PSG splashed out £34 million on him as they began building a squad of stars to match the best in Europe!

26
David Villa

£34.2 million

Valencia to Barcelona

May 2010

Villa is one of the 21st century's greatest strikers and Spain's all-time top goalscorer, but he had to wait until he was 28 years old before getting his dream move to Barcelona! His goals and assists in the big matches mean he'll go down as a legend!

25
Gonzalo Higuain

£34.5 million

Real Madrid to Napoli

July 2013

Real were starting a summer clear-out with the club set to sign Gareth Bale, and the man to make way was Higuain. The lethal striker, who had fallen behind Karim Benzema in The Bernabeu pecking order, jumped at the chance to join Serie A giants Napoli!

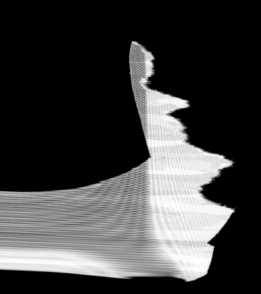

24 Lucas Moura

£35 million

Sao Paulo to PSG

August 2012

The Brazil trickster came close to joining every big club in Europe in 2011 and 2012! But it was PSG who matched Sao Paulo's huge valuation before Man. United and Inter Milan could blink, and the skilful 19-year-old winger agreed to move to Paris!

23 Thiago Silva

£35 million

AC Milan to PSG

July 2012

The baby-faced Brazilian looked set for a long future at AC Milan when he signed a new five-year deal on July 2, 2012. But PSG proved that 12 days is a long time in football by announcing they had signed the world's best defender on July 14. Wow!

22 Radamel Falcao

ATLETICO MADRID'S RECORD SIGNING!

£35 million

Porto to Atletico Madrid

August 2011

Falcao arrived at Porto as a 23-year-old and made it his mission to tear up the Portuguese league! Two seasons of goal-filled destruction later, and Atletico jumped at the chance of smashing their own transfer record by adding him to their slick squad!

21 Andy Carroll

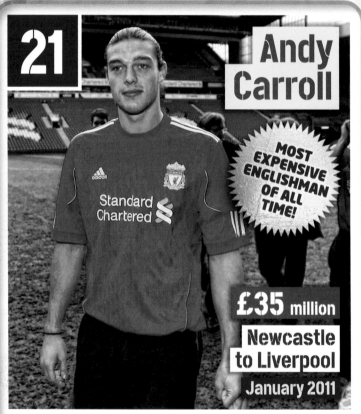

MOST EXPENSIVE ENGLISHMAN OF ALL TIME!

£35 million

Newcastle to Liverpool

January 2011

The Reds might have got their hands on Carroll for just £20 million if news of Fernando Torres' £50 million sale to Chelsea hadn't leaked! Newcastle knew Liverpool had cash and desperately needed a striker, so refused to sell for less than £35 million!

20 Hernan Crespo

£35.5 million

Parma to Lazio

July 2000

SERIE A'S RECORD SIGNING!

Lazio won the double in 1999-2000, and manager Sven-Goran Eriksson celebrated by breaking the world transfer record! He swapped £16 million of cash and £19.5 million of his players for Crespo, who won the Serie A Golden Boot in his first season!

Porto to Monaco

July 2013

James' first entry on MATCH's Top 50 countdown sees him swap the quiet life of Portugal for the mega-rich principality of Monaco and become Ligue 1's second most expensive star in the process! He was a rapidly-growing talent who was about to go global!

15

Hulk

£38.5 million

Porto to Zenit St. Petersburg

September 2012

Hulk waited, and waited, and waited for a Prem, La Liga or Serie A club to bid for him in 2012, but Porto's huge asking price put them all off! Instead, Porto agreed a deal with Zenit and the Brazil powerhouse has been bossing the Russian league ever since!

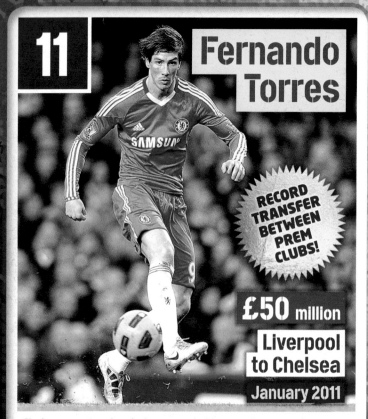

11

Fernando Torres

RECORD TRANSFER BETWEEN PREM CLUBS!

£50 million

Liverpool to Chelsea

January 2011

Chelsea constantly tried to wrestle Liverpool's star striker away from Anfield in 2010 and 2011, but it took a record-breaking Prem fee to get the deal done! Torres' first match for The Blues came a week later against Liverpool, which Chelsea lost 1-0!

…tenham Years

…azy to think Bale is
…on this list, because
…early sold him to West
…or £3 million in 2009!
…attled back, got in the
…am and started ripping
…ers to shreds. Legend!

…eal Madrid Plan

…new Cristiano Ronaldo
…one of Bale's big foot…
…es and thought th…
…k well together…
…team! Spurs…
…rld-record…
…ped up t…

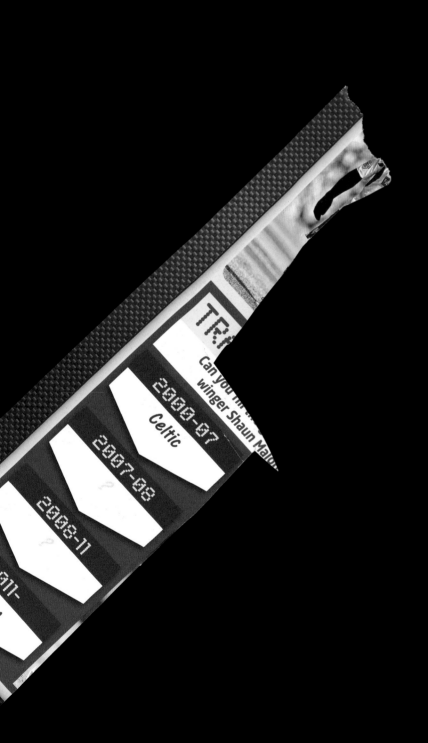

17

Sergio Aguero

MAN. CITY'S RECORD SIGNING!

12

David Luiz

MOST EXPENSIVE DEFENDER OF ALL TIME!

DAVID LUIZ

£50 million

Chelsea to PSG

June 2014

...n pulled off a miracle by convincing PSG to pay £50 million
...efender who'd forgotten how to defend! Dodgy displays
...3-14 relegated the centre-back to The Blues' bench, but
...n't care and he's now the most expensive defender ever!

9 Edinson Cavani

LIGUE 1'S RECORD SIGNING!

£55 million

Napoli to PSG

July 2013

PSG had built an attacking team packed with skill, creativity and wondergoals, but they still needed a lethal penalty-box predator to complete the jigsaw! Cavani had scored 78 league goals in three seasons for Napoli, and was quickly handed a five-year deal!

8 Kaka

£56 million

AC Milan to Real Madrid

June 2009

Real smashed the world transfer record to sign the best player of the late 2000s! Kaka's touch, trickery and goalscoring ability were on another level in Milan, but the signing of Cristiano Ronaldo and a bad knee injury meant the Brazil legend struggled in Madrid!

Gareth Bale

£85.3 million

ottenham to Real Madrid

eptember 2013

7 Zlatan Ibrahimovic

MOST EXPENSIVE SWEDE OF ALL TIME!

£57 million

Inter Milan to Barcelona

July 2009

Barça had historically avoided bank-busting signings, but that all changed when Pep Guardiola realised he could sign Zlat! The most naturally-talented player of his time moved to Spain in exchange for £17 million-rated striker Samuel Eto'o plus £40 million

5 James Rodriguez

£71 million

Monaco to Real Madrid

July 2014

Real Madrid's 2014 transfer mission was to find a world-class midfielder who could handle playing between Cristiano Ronaldo and Gareth Bale in their attacking midfield three! J-Rod stepped up to dominate Brazil 2014 and Real had their new Galactico!

BIG MATCH! QUIZ
FOOTBALL LEALGUE SPECIAL

FLASHBACK!

Which class Ipswich star will want to forget this dodgy pic from 2006?

WHO

Work out the mystery star from these three clues!

...m a tricky ...riker who ...e to fame ...t Leeds!

...played a ...eason for 2010-11!

...banging ...despite ...my 30s!

...R!
...ey's career?

THE NICKNAME GAME!

Match these Football League clubs with their crazy nicknames!

Sheff. United	Bradford	Reading	Swindon
1	2	3	4
A	B	C	D
The Bantams	The Robins	The Royals	The Blades

GROUNDED!

Which massive club plays its home games at this awesome stadium?

inverness ccs

Luis Suarez

£75 million
Liverpool to Barcelona
July 2014

Barcelona Plan

The Uruguay hitman will help Barça become the most-feared team in club footy! They need to be much more dangerous in Champo League and El Clasico games, and teaming Suarez up with Messi should do that!

Cristiano Ronaldo

£80 million
Man. United to Real Madrid
July 2009

Real Madrid Plan

Real were desperate to become the world's best club again, and they knew they needed to sign Ronaldo to do that! His £80 million deal was the start of their journey to tenth Champo League win!

Dream Team!

Ewood Park's ex-England stopper!

Can you work out which players are in MATCH's Football League XI?

GK
 Nuye

Leeds' 2012-13 Player Of The Year!
RB — Raven

Bournemouth star who sorts out dinner!
CB — P.jones

Bluebirds giant and former Coventry rock!
CB — Dao v

25-year-old attack-minded Scottish Ram!
LB — G.Shinn

Middlesbrough and Ghana speedster!
RW — Grorg

Wolves' ex-Dundee and Burnley warrior!
CM — Ronal

Forest's £1 million former Walsall wonderkid!
LW — bale

26-year-old Watford goal machine!
ST — M day

Huddersfield and Bermuda pocket rocket!
ST — Messi

The Canaries' lethal SPL winner!
ST — Persie

the PRICE is Right!

Match stars with the money their current club paid for them.

1. Jordan Rhodes *Blackburn*
2. Bakary Sako *Wolves*
3. Matt Mills *Bolton*
4. Ross McCormack *Fulham*

A. £2 Million
B. £11 Million
C. £8 Million
D. £3 Million

Alex Tettey Norwich

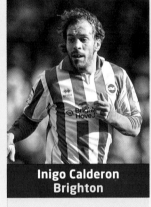
Inigo Calderon Brighton

EUROPEAN INVADERS!

Which countries do these class foreign FL stars call home?

Tim Hoogland Fulham

Aron Gunnarsson Cardiff

DERBY RIVALS!

Match up the two teams who call each other 'The Enemy!'

1. Yeovil
2. Preston
3. Millwall
4. Derby

A. Nott'm Forest
B. Bristol City
C. Charlton
D. Blackpool

CRAZY KIT!

Which Champo team wore this dodgy third kit in 2008-09?

ANSWERS ON PAGE 91

RU 2 BROTHERS?

Check out the best lookalikes of the year!

CHRISTOPHER WALKEN
HOLLYWOOD ACTOR

LOUIS VAN GAAL
MAN. UNITED GAFFER

ANDRE SCHURRLE
CHELSEA

NICKY BYRNE
WESTLIFE

RAYMONDO THE HONEYBADGER
SOUTH AFRICA

ELLIOTT WRIGHT
TOWIE

MATHIEU DEBUCHY
ARSENAL

JAVIER MASCHERANO
BARCELONA

GRANIT XHAKA
BORUSSIA MONCHENGLADBACH

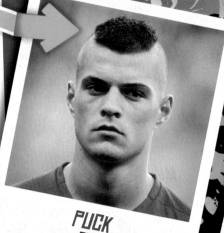

PUCK
GLEE

AXEL WITSEL
ZENIT

PHOENIX TAYLOR
WATERLOO ROAD

THE LIGHTNING SQUAD

Speed Machine!

The quality Blues winger skins full-backs week-in, week-out with his rapid pace! Hazard combines lightning-quick runs with eye-popping dribbling skills and jaw-dropping tricks to totally ruin opposition defences!

Eden's Stats!

Five-yard bursts	86
Weaving runs	93
Long sprints	90
Dribbling control	98
Top speed	91

He should be called...

The Superbike!

EDEN
HAZARD
CHELSEA

NO.3 LUIS

PREM NET RIPPER!

Suarez won last season's Premier League Golden Boot with 31 goals - no player has scored more than that in a single 38-game season!

LIVERPOOL LEGEND!

In 2013-14, he became the first Reds player to score 30 or more league goals in a season since legendary striker Ian Rush in 1986-87!

WAG WATCH!

Luis lives in Barcelona with his wife Sofia Balbi and their two footy-mad children - daughter Delfina and son Benjamin.

LUIS' FANS!

The Barça and Uruguay megastar has over nine million likes on Facebook and nearly four million followers on Twitter!

MATCH MEGASTAR!

Luis is the only player in history to win MATCH's Premier League Player Of The Month award three times in a single season!

SUAREZ'S ROYAL PATH!

1987
A king is born!

2001
Joins Nacional's youth team in Uruguay aged 14!

2005
Debuts for Nacional, then joins Groningen just a year later!

2007
Signs for Dutch giants Ajax for £7 million!

SUAREZ

NATIONAL HERO!

Suarez is Uruguay's all-time top scorer with 40 goals in 79 games, and was Player Of The Tournament as his country won the 2011 Copa America!

MEGA TRANSFERS!

He's one of just three stars – along with James Rodriguez and Zlatan Ibrahimovic – whose combined career transfer fees total over £100 million. Legend!

AWARD HOGGER!

His trophy cabinet must be jam-packed! He won last season's PFA, FWA and Prem Player Of The Year awards, Premier League Golden Boot and European Golden Shoe!

2010
Fires Uruguay to fourth place at World Cup 2010!

2010
Wins the Dutch Footballer Of The Year award!

2011
Moves to Liverpool for £22.8 million!

2011
Wins the Copa America with Uruguay!

2012
Wins the League Cup – his first trophy in England!

2014
Bags 31 Prem goals and PFA Player Of The Year award!

2014
Joins Barcelona for a monster £75 million!

KING OF SKILLS!

EXPERT FOOTY BRAIN!

Suarez is always aware of what's happening around him and has the vision to play a killer pass or shoot from anywhere! He wasn't fully fit at Brazil 2014, but his brain helped him make defence-destroying runs for both goals against England!

SCORE: 97/100

MASSIVE PASSION!

There aren't many players with more passion than Luis! He gives 100% every time he steps onto the pitch and will do anything to help his team win – which sometimes gets him into trouble! His epic work-rate, desire and enthusiasm are great to watch!

SCORE: 99/100

EAGLE-EYED SHOOTING!

Suarez scores all types of goals – net-ripping half-volleys, cheeky lobs, slick finesse finishes and efforts with the outside of his foot! He bagged 208 goals in just 329 games for Groningen, Ajax and Liverpool before joining Barcelona last summer!

SCORE: 94/100

JAW-DROPPING TRICKS!

The Barcelona hero's technique is off the charts and he has bags of confidence! He loves busting out body swerves, clever drops of the shoulder, stepovers and nutmegs! It's almost impossible to stop him, Neymar and Messi from making La Liga defenders look silly!

SCORE: 94/100

DAZZLING DRIBBLING!

Luis is one of the best dribblers in the world! He loves taking on defenders and his mix of close control and lightning pace is unstoppable! Last season he completed 93 successful dribbles - the second most in the Premier League behind Eden Hazard!

SCORE: 93/100

MEGA WORDSEARCH!

Can you find 40 class 2014 summer signings in this giant grid?

Alex AC Milan	**Fabregas** Chelsea	**Kettings** Crystal Palace	**Morata** Juventus
Aspas Sevilla	**Ferdinand** QPR	**Kroos** Real Madrid	**Pantilimon** Sunderland
Barry Everton	**Finnbogason** Real Sociedad	**Lambert** Liverpool	**Sam** Schalke
Bojan Stoke	**Garay** Zenit	**Lescott** West Brom	**Senderos** Aston Villa
Buttner Dynamo Moscow	**Gomis** Swansea	**Lewandowski** Bayern Munich	**Snodgrass** Hull
Caballero Man. City	**Gordon** Celtic	**Luiz** PSG	**Suarez** Barcelona
Cabella Newcastle	**Heitinga** Hertha Berlin	**Mandzukic** Atletico Madrid	**Tadic** Southampton
Cole Roma	**Herrera** Man. United	**Markovic** Liverpool	**Ulloa** Leicester
Debuchy Arsenal	**Immobile** Borussia Dortmund	**Martins Indi** Porto	**Valencia** West Ham
Drmic Bayer Leverkusen	**Jutkiewicz** Burnley	**Michu** Napoli	**Vorm** Tottenham

ANSWERS ON PAGE 91

THE LIGHTNING SQUAD

Speed Machine!

Kun probably wouldn't win a 100-metre race against The Lightning Squad's very quickest stars, but not many of his rivals would match him for pure acceleration! The City star's 0-20mph is something special!

Sergio's Stats!

Five-yard bursts	96
Weaving runs	91
Long sprints	83
Dribbling control	94
Top speed	90

He should be called...

The Powerboat!

SERGIO
AGUERO
MAN. CITY

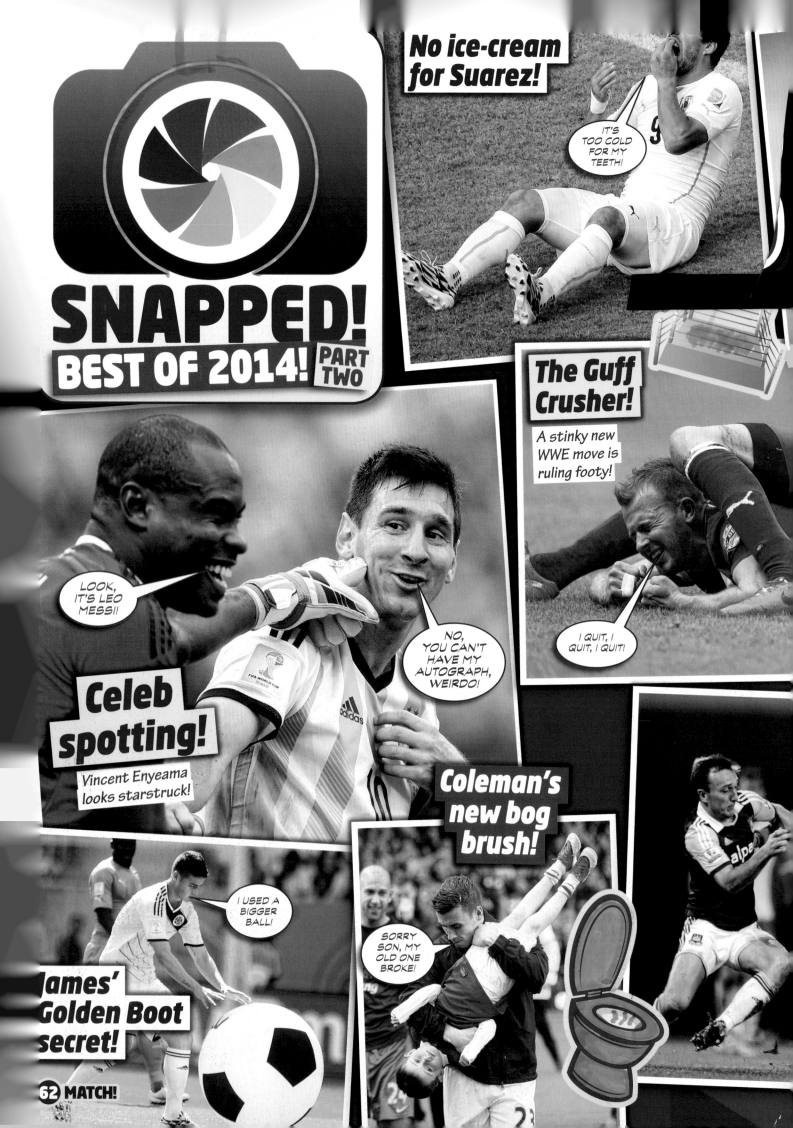

BIG MATCH! QUIZ

WORLD CUP SPECIAL

FLASHBACK!

Can you name this Croatia superstar from Brazil 2014's opening game?

5 QUESTIONS ON...

GERMANY

DEUTSCHER FUSSBALL-BUND

1 Who scored Germany's first goal of Brazil 2014 - Thomas Muller, Miroslav Klose or Mats Hummels?

Thomas

2 Who bagged Germany's winning goal in the World Cup final against Argentina?

G.t

3 Name the legendary gaffer who managed the 2014 World Cup winners!

4 Mesut Ozil, Lukas Podolski and which other Arsenal star was in Germany's squad?

5 Which country did they knock out in the last 16 - Algeria, France or Brazil?

CAMERA SHY!

Name the players trying to hide their faces during the World Cup final!

CL☺SE-UP!

Which Brazil 2014 heroes have we zoomed in on?

1.

2.

3.

4.

SPOT THE BALL!

Mark where you think the ball is in this awesome action pic!

A B C D E F G H I J K
1 2 3 4 5 6 7 8 9 10 11 12 13 14 15 16 17 18 19

BRAZIL 2014 STARS!

Which countries did these heroes shine for in Brazil?

1. Gary Medel

2. Blaise Matuidi

3. Guillermo Ochoa

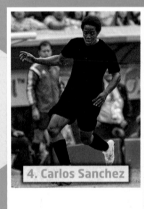
4. Carlos Sanchez

MATCH! WINNER!

Who scored Argentina's winner against Belgium in the quarter-finals?

CRAZY KIT!

Which massive country wore this bonkers kit in Brazil?

usa

ANSWERS ON PAGE 91

PREM SUPER CLUBS!

MATCH adds up the trophies of the most successful clubs in English footy to answer the hottest question of all - who really is the biggest?

SUNDERLAND
League titles: 6
FA Cups: 2 ★ **League Cups:** 0
TOTAL: 36 points

10TH

The Black Cats won three titles in the 1800s! They're English footy's forgotten powerhouse!

TOTTENHAM
League titles: 2
FA Cups: 8 ★ **League Cups:** 4
TOTAL: 38 points

9TH

Spurs have big support and a class cup record, but two league titles is a bit disappointing!

MAN. CITY
League titles: 4
FA Cups: 5 ★ **League Cups:** 3
TOTAL: 38 points

8TH

City have spent most of their history in the shadow of their red rivals, but four trophies in recent years has started to change that!

NEWCASTLE
League titles: 4
FA Cups: 6 ★ **League Cups:** 0
TOTAL: 38 points

7TH

Newcastle had won three titles by 1910, but haven't bagged a trophy since 1955! To be giants again they need to sort that out!

CHELSEA
League titles: 4
FA Cups: 7 ★ **League Cups:** 4
TOTAL: 45 points

6TH

The Blues wouldn't have made this list before Roman Abramovich arrived, but nine trophies in ten years has turned them into a super club!

EVERTON
League titles: 9
FA Cups: 5 ★ **League Cups:** 0
TOTAL: 60 points

5TH

The Toffees have won more league titles than Chelsea and Man. City combined, but no League Cup wins mean they miss out on the top four!

ASTON VILLA
League titles: 7
FA Cups: 7 ★ **League Cups:** 5
TOTAL: 61 points

4TH

Villa's trophy total was up there with Liverpool, Man. United and Arsenal's at the start of the 1980s. But their lack of league titles since then means they're now miles behind the top three!

ARSENAL
League titles: 13
FA Cups: 11 ★ **League Cups:** 2
TOTAL: 100 points

3RD

The Gunners are probably the most consistent club in English footy! They've won league titles in the 1930s, 40s, 50s, 70s, 80s, 90s and 00s, so expect them to grab the trophy back soon!

LIVERPOOL
League titles: 18
FA Cups: 7 ★ **League Cups:** 8
TOTAL: 119 points

2ND

Liverpool fans will be gutted to come second in our countdown, but it was close! The Reds bossed the 1970s and 80s with 18 English trophies and their new wonderkids want more!

BIG BOYS!

MAN. UNITED
League titles: 20
FA Cups: 11 ★ **League Cups:** 4
TOTAL: 137 points

1ST

United are the most successful club in English footy history, and have one man to thank for making that happen! Gaffer Sir Alex Ferguson won 22 of United's 35 trophies. What a legend!

Dribb
Top speed

He should be

The Missi

RAHEEM
STERLING
LIVERPOOL

CRISTIA

GOAL KING!

He's hit 177 La Liga goals in his first five full seasons at Real Madrid! That's an average of more than 35 goals a season. Bonkers!

BALLON D'OR HOLDER!

Ronaldo stopped Barça's Lionel Messi winning five Ballon d'Ors in a row by grabbing the 2013 prize!

BLING BOOTS!

He gets £14.1 million a year from Nike and has his own CR7 boot collection with the mega sports brand!

CR 7

NEY HINE!

massive deals with AG Heuer, on Soccer s more!

DO'S PATH!

1985
A king is born!

1997
Passes a three-day trial at Sporting Lisbon with ease!

2003
Man Of The Match in Sporting's friendly against Man. United!

2003
The Red Devils sign Ronaldo for £12.2 million!

CASH CRAZY!

Ronaldo signed a new five-year deal with Real Madrid last season, which is worth £288,000 a week!

WAG WATCH!

Russian model Irina Shayk has been Cristiano's girlfriend since 2010 and joined him in Nike's 2014 World Cup advert!

2004
Stars at Euro 2004, but Portugal lose 1-0 to Greece in the final!

2008
Helps United beat Chelsea in the Champions League final!

2012
Bags 46 goals as Real Madrid win La Liga title!

2004
Scores as United beat Millwall in the FA Cup Final!

2007
Wins Prem title and PFA Player Of The Year award!

2009
Joins Real Madrid in world record £80 million deal!

2014
Nets as Real beat Atletico Madrid 4-1 in CL final!

MAZY DRIBBLING!

Ron's become such a massive goal machine, people forget how good his dribbling is! He made his name at Sporting Lisbon with his silky wing skills, and he's still got those tekkers today! He bursts past full-backs with speed, close control and massive confidence!

SCORE: 96/100

NET-BUSTING FINISHING!

Ronaldo has stats that make you rub your eyes in disbelief! He netted 17 goals in 11 Champions League games last season and bagged 31 times in La Liga! He's ice-cool in front of goal, never rushes his one-on-ones and always finds the corners!

SCORE: 98/100

Speed Machine!

Dyer is like a little hare who bursts around the pitch with bags of pace and energy! Full-backs can't rest for a second when the Swansea speedster is around, because his pace can change any match!

Nathan's Stats!

Five-yard bursts	93
Weaving runs	96
Long sprints	87
Dribbling control	89
Top speed	92

He should be called...

The Pocket Rocket!

NATHAN
DYER
SWANSEA

MY SUPER

RAHEEM STERLING
LIVERPOOL

RAZZA SAYS: "My biggest strengths are my pace and my dribbling. When I did athletics at school I could run 100 metres in 10.99 seconds, so I think I'm quite nippy! I also like to express myself on the ball and create chances for the team. I've got alright technique and a few tricks which I use to unbalance my opponents!"

BEN DAVIES
TOTTENHAM

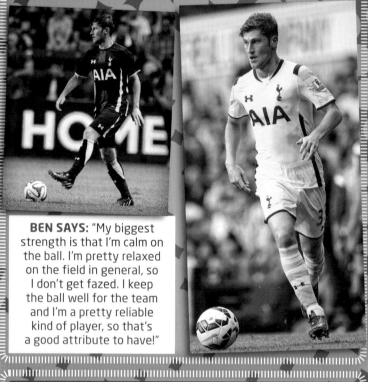

BEN SAYS: "My biggest strength is that I'm calm on the ball. I'm pretty relaxed on the field in general, so I don't get fazed. I keep the ball well for the team and I'm a pretty reliable kind of player, so that's a good attribute to have!"

ROMELU LUKAKU
EVERTON

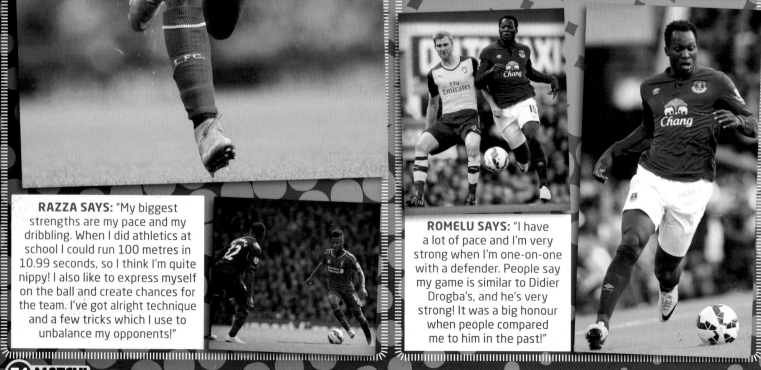

ROMELU SAYS: "I have a lot of pace and I'm very strong when I'm one-on-one with a defender. People say my game is similar to Didier Drogba's, and he's very strong! It was a big honour when people compared me to him in the past!"

POWER!

CALUM CHAMBERS
ARSENAL

CALUM SAYS: "My biggest strength is breaking forward from right-back. I like to get over the halfway line, make crosses and help the team attack. I'm also 6ft 1$\frac{1}{2}$ins tall and I'd describe myself as a powerful runner, so that helps a lot too!"

NATHAN REDMOND
NORWICH

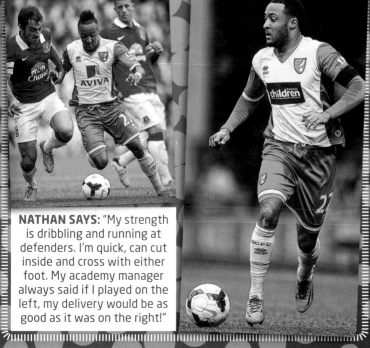

NATHAN SAYS: "My strength is dribbling and running at defenders. I'm quick, can cut inside and cross with either foot. My academy manager always said if I played on the left, my delivery would be as good as it was on the right!"

ANDRE SCHURRLE
CHELSEA

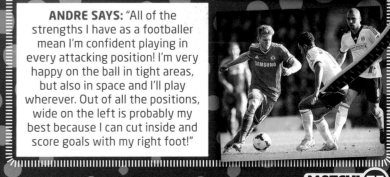

ANDRE SAYS: "All of the strengths I have as a footballer mean I'm confident playing in every attacking position! I'm very happy on the ball in tight areas, but also in space and I'll play wherever. Out of all the positions, wide on the left is probably my best because I can cut inside and score goals with my right foot!"

ROSS BARKLEY
EVERTON

ROSS SAYS: "I like playing off the striker and I'm not afraid to get on the ball under pressure and drive forward with it! The No.10 position suits me, but I can play in any of the attacking midfield places of a 4-2-3-1 formation. I just like getting on the ball and putting the defenders in tricky positions!"

BEN FOSTER
WEST BROM

BEN SAYS: "Dominating the penalty area is a part of the game that I really enjoy, and I think I'm decent at it! I always stay aware of which players are around me and make sure my feet are right so I can reach the ball first. I'm quite tall too, 6ft 4ins, so I've always believed I will catch crosses!"

ALEX OXLADE-CHAMB.
ARSENAL

THE OX SAYS: "When the game kicks off, my aim is to bring something extra to the field and try to 'Wow' people! I'm all about doing something that not too many other people are doing. The most important thing is to get the basics right, but I'm very happy if I can do something special!"

RICKIE LAMBERT
LIVERPOOL

RICKIE SAYS: "I'm a ten out of ten for penalties! For me, a penalty kick is as simple as anything you'll have to deal with in your career. It's a free shot from 12 yards! If you keep it that simple, then you're always favourite! If you complicate it you're only going to help the keeper, so I don't!"

JUNIOR HOILETT
QPR

JACK BUTLAND
STOKE

JACK SAYS: "I'd like to think shot-stopping is my biggest strength. As a keeper, your positioning and handling have to be on-point because that's the key part of your job. I'd like to think that part of my game, and being able to get down quickly and near the top corners when I dive, are my strongest points!"

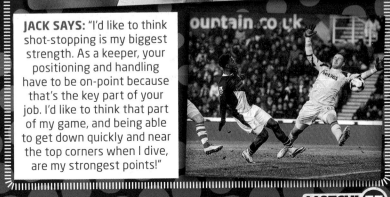

BRAZIL 2014 SCRAPBOOK!

MATCH takes a look back at the biggest stats, facts, pics and stories from the awesome 2014 WORLD CUP!

GROUP STAGES

SUPERVAN!

Robin van Persie's epic acrobatic diving header is the highlight as Holland hammer holders Spain 5-1!

TOP 5 GOALSCORERS!
1. James Rodriguez - 6
2. Thomas Muller - 5
3= Lionel Messi - 4
3= Neymar - 4
3= Robin van Persie - 4

GET THE PARTY STARTED!

J-Lo and Pitbull kick off the opening ceremony in style, then Neymar steals the show as Brazil beat Croatia 3-1!

SUPER MARIO LANDS!

15.4 million Brits watch England's opening game against Italy on TV, but Mario Balotelli spoils the party with an ice-cool winning header!

MULLER NICE!

Pepe loses his cool and gets sent off as Germany hero Thomas Muller hammers a hat-trick past Portugal!

2.7

There was an average of 2.7 goals per match over the 64-game tournament!

TOP 5 GOALS CONCEDED!
1. Brazil - 14
2= Australia - 9
2= Cameroon - 9
4. Honduras - 8
5. Algeria - 7
*Three more teams conceded seven goals

JOHN JUMPS FOR JOY!

John Brooks becomes an internet sensation after scoring USA's winner against Ghana! His totally shocked face went global!

LEO THE LEGEND!

Lionel Messi silences the critics who have a dig at his World Cup record by scoring a stunner against Bosnia in Argentina's first game!

TOP 5 MOST SHOTS!
1. Karim Benzema - 32
2. Angel di Maria - 25
3. Cristiano Ronaldo - 23
4. Lionel Messi - 22
5. Xherdan Shaqiri - 21

MEXICAN SPIDERMAN!

Goalkeeper Guillermo Ochoa shuts out the hosts with tons of wondersaves to help Mexico grab a 0-0 draw with Brazil!

111

Brazil had the most shots during the tournament with 111 - six more than runners-up Argentina!

CAHILL'S WONDER STRIKE!

Australia's Tim Cahill made all of our jaws drop after slamming an unstoppable volley past Holland – with his weak foot!

SUAREZ SILENCES ENGLAND!

We all feared Luis Suarez was going to hurt England, and he didn't disappoint his fans! His deadly double helped Uruguay win 2-1!

4,157

Germany completed 4,157 of their 5,084 attempted passes in Brazil – that's a success rate of 82%!

TOP 5 GOALS SCORED!
1. Germany - 18
2. Holland - 15
3. Colombia - 12
4. Brazil - 11
5. France - 10

SPAIN SHOCK!

World Cup holders Spain crash out of the World Cup after being taught a footy lesson and losing 2-0 to slick South Americans Chile at The Maracana!

TOP 5 MOST SAVES!
1. Tim Howard - 27
2. Manuel Neuer - 25
3. Rais M'Bolhi - 23
4. Diego Benaglio - 22
5. Vincent Enyeama - 21
*Two more goalkeepers made 21 saves

BENZEMA STUNS SWISS!

Karim Benzema scores one, grabs two assists, misses a penalty and even has a late goal disallowed as France demolish Switzerland 5-2!

TOP 5 MOST ASSISTS!
1= Juan Cuadrado - 4
1= Toni Kroos - 4
3. Thomas Muller - 3
4= Karim Benzema - 2
4= Daley Blind - 2
*Four more players got two assists

MAGIC MIGUEL!
Mad Mexico gaffer Miguel Herrera busts out some bonkers celebrations as his team beat Croatia 3-1 to qualify for the knockout stages!

BITE NIGHT!
Luis Suarez becomes the most talked-about man on the planet after biting Italy defender Giorgio Chiellini! Crazy!

12
Holland striker Robin van Persie was caught offside 12 times - four more than anyone else!

ICE-COOL SAMARAS!
Georgios Samaras proves he's got nerves of steel by scoring a last-gasp penalty against Ivory Coast to send Greece into the last 16!

SAMBA STARS ARE SPOT-ON!
Brazil cling on to their World Cup dreams by surviving an extra-time scare against Chile, before knocking them out 3-2 on pens!

LAST 16

TOP 5 BIGGEST FOULERS!
1. Marouane Fellaini - 19
2. Robin van Persie - 18
3. Reza Ghoochannejhad - 17
4. Luiz Gustavo - 15
5. Christian Bolanos - 14

*Two more players committed 14 fouls

HOT ROD!

James Rodriguez proves he's the star of the World Cup with a dynamite double against Uruguay, including a legendary volley!

PURE KLAAS!

Holland score two priceless late goals, including a cool stoppage-time penalty from Klaas-Jan Huntelaar, to knock Mexico out in the last 16!

TOP 5 MOST TACKLES!
1. Oscar - 30
2. Javier Mascherano - 22
3. Mehrdad Pooladi - 19
4= Kyle Beckerman - 18
4= Benedikt Howedes - 18

BRILL BELGIUM!

Kevin de Bruyne and Romelu Lukaku finally beat USA keeper Tim Howard to help Belgium reach the quarters!

QUARTER-FINALS

MATS THE WAY TO DO IT!

Germany win their all-European quarter-final with France after rock-solid defender Mats Hummels flicks a wicked header off the crossbar and in!

SEMI-FINALS

KHEDIRA

BRAZIL 1 - 7 GERMANY

SONY

SEVENTH HEAVEN!

Germany send shockwaves around the planet after crushing hosts Brazil 7-1 in the first semi-final! Toni Kroos and Andre Schurrle score twice, while Thomas Muller, Miroslav Klose and Sami Khedira also rip net!

ARGENTINA'S PENALTY POWER!

Argentina reach the World Cup final by beating Holland 4-2 on penalties in the semis after 120 minutes of boring action!

MASCHERANO

14

Brazil bagged the most yellow cards in the tournament with 14! The hosts committed 123 fouls, too!

LUIZ THE LEGEND!

David Luiz sends over 200 million Brazilians crazy after scoring an unstoppable match-winning free-kick against Colombia in the quarter-finals!

83,957

That's how many metres Gemany legend Thomas Muller covered during the tournament! He could be a marathon runner!

THE FINAL

GOTZE'S GOLDEN GOAL!

Mario Gotze settles a tense World Cup final with a classic left-foot volley to help Germany beat Argentina 1-0!

JUNIOR SAYS: "Dribbling is one of my key skills. I like to keep the ball close to my feet when I run at defenders, so they don't know what I'm going to do next. I also like using the inside and outside of my left and right foot. I'm hard to knock off the ball as I've got a low centre of gravity and stocky legs!"

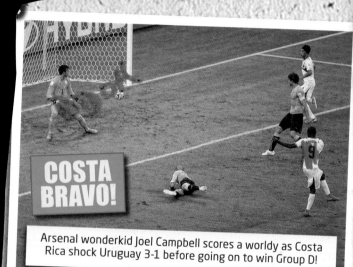

COSTA BRAVO!

Arsenal wonderkid Joel Campbell scores a worldy as Costa Rica shock Uruguay 3-1 before going on to win Group D!

NO.5 LIONE

BALLON D'OR LEGEND!

Messi is the only footy star in history to win the Ballon d'Or award four times!

...G WATCH!

...girlfriend is called
...onella Roccuzzo
...they have a son
...er called Thiago.

REC... BREA...

He netted 73 ... in 2011-12, whic... the biggest season total in European club footy history!

KING OF FACEBOOK!

His Facebook page has nearly 69 million likes! That's even more than MATCH!

...ESSI'S ...YAL PATH!

1987
A king is born!

1998
Signs for Barcelona on a paper napkin aged just 11!

FCB

2004
Makes La Liga debut and wins the title in his first season!

2007
Becomes the first player in 12 seasons to score a hat-trick in El Clasico!

Speed Machine!

...d bursts...
...uickly...
...goin...
...id!

...should be called

The Greyhound!

GABRIEL
AGBONLAHOR
ASTON VILLA

L MESSI

UNITED'S WORST NIGHTMARE!

Messi bagged in both the 2009 and 2011 Champo League Finals against Man. United!

EL CLASICO KING!

Leo's scored the most goals in El Clasico history! By the end of 2013-14 he'd netted 21 times against arch-rivals Real Madrid, including 14 in La Liga and two in the Champions League!

MONEYBAGS!

He pockets £13.6 million a year from Adidas and has bumper deals with Gillette, EA Sports and Pepsi too!

NET-BUSTER!

Leo became the youngest player in history to score 200 La Liga goals – he was just 25 years old!

2009
Bags a header in Champo League final against Man. United!

2011
Destroys United again in the 2011 Champo League Final at Wembley!

2013
Bags his fourth Ballon d'Or trophy in a row!

2007
Nets a famous wondergoal in the Copa del Rey against Getafe!

2009
Wins his first Ballon d'Or trophy ahead of Cristiano Ronaldo and Xavi!

2012
Ends 2011-12 with

2014
Plays in his first World Cup final!

INCREDIBLE ACCELERATION!

Messi might not hit the same top speed as some of his rivals, but not many stars can match his electric acceleration! He bursts away from defenders like a hungry cheetah chasing a gazelle when he takes off! It's a sudden explosion of pace!

SCORE: 98/100

DEMON DRIBBLER!

The Barcelona superstar is the greatest dribbler in footy history! The ball sticks to his foot like he's got Superglue on his boots, he always takes extra touches before shooting or passing to confuse defenders and he can change direction in a split-second!

SCORE: 100/100

machine - the Argentina genius is an unselfish assist king too! He's bagged 38 La Liga assists in his last three seasons, and always picks out a team-mate with a killer pass if he's in a better goalscoring position!

SCORE: 95/100

SUPREME SHOOTING!

Messi has re-written the rule book for statistics! Scoring 20 goals a season used to be pretty good, but Leo has changed all that by smashing home 189 La Liga strikes and 50 Champions League goals in his last five full seasons! His left foot is a lethal weapon!

SCORE: 99/100

FANTASTIC FREE-KICKS!

Messi's free-kick technique is off the charts! He wraps his left foot around dead balls like a legend and the mix of pace, dip, accuracy and power makes them impossible for goalkeepers to stop! He could bend one round a 30ft wall and still find the net if he wanted to!

SCORE: 93/100

Speed Machine!

The wing wizard's combination of balance and acceleration means he sprints like he's got rockets in his boots! Once The Hammers hero has galloped to the byline, he's also one of the best crossers in the business!

Matt's Stats!

Five-yard bursts	92
Weaving runs	89
Long sprints	90
Dribbling control	86
Top speed	93

He should be called...

The Speeding Bullet!

MATT JARVIS
WEST HAM

QUIZ ANSWERS!

Premier League Special — Pages 22-23

Who Am I?: Daniel Sturridge.

5 Questions On Alexis Sanchez:
1. £33 million; 2. Udinese; 3. Two – against Australia & Brazil; 4. No.17; 5. True.

Flipped: Mauricio Pochettino.

Soccer Scrabble: Enner Valencia.

Premier League Brain-Buster:
1. Leicester, Burnley & QPR; 2. Two; 3. 1992; 4. Swansea; 5. Third; 6. Man. United – Old Trafford; 7. Three; 8. Man. City – 102 goals; 9. Seven – Arsenal, Aston Villa, Chelsea, Everton, Liverpool, Man. United & Tottenham; 10. Angel di Maria.

Wicked Wordfit — Page 28

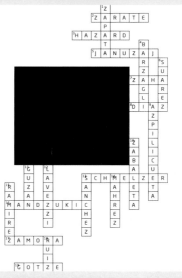

Champions League Special — Pages 34-35

Footy At The Films: Gareth Bale.

Bogus Badge: Olympiakos.

Odd One Out: AC Milan.

Back To The Future: Adam Lallana.

Caught On Camera: Jurgen Klopp, Diego Simeone & Laurent Blanc.

5 Questions On The Champions League:
1. Real Madrid; 2. Berlin's Olympic Stadium; 3. Five – Aston Villa, Chelsea, Liverpool, Man. United & Nottingham Forest; 4. Raul; 5. Adidas.

Guess The Winners:
2014 – Real Madrid; 2012 – Chelsea; 2010 – Inter Milan; 2008 – Man. United.

Spot The Sponsor: 1. Atletico Madrid;

---

2. Bayern Munich; 3. Juventus; 4. Chelsea; 5. Ajax; 6. Barcelona.

Bonkers Fans: Bayern Munich.

Crossword Crunch — Page 37

Across: 2. Rome; 5. Norwich; 7. Chevrolet; 12. Cristiano Ronaldo; 14. Benteke; 16. Fabregas; 18. Sevilla; 19. Diego; 20. Maracana; 21. Puma; 22. Clarets; 23. Athletic Bilbao.

Down: 1. France; 3. Portugal; 4. QPR; 6. Hull; 8. Bundesliga; 9. James Rodriguez; 10. Southampton; 11. Costa Rica; 13. Millwall; 14. Ba; 15. Vlaar; 17. Adidas; 21. Posh.

Football League Special — Pages 52-53

Flashback: Stephen Hunt.

Who Am I?: Jermaine Beckford.

The Nickname Game: 1-D; 2-A; 3-C; 4-B.

Transfer Tracker:
2007-08 – Aston Villa; 2008-11 – Celtic.

Grounded: Sheff. Wednesday – Hillsborough.

Dream Team: GK – Paul Robinson; RB – Sam Byram; CB – Steve Cook; CB – Ben Turner; LB – Craig Forsyth; RW – Albert Adomah; CM – Kevin McDonald; LW – Jamie Paterson; ST – Troy Deeney; ST – Nahki Wells; ST – Gary Hooper.

The Price Is Right: 1-C; 2-D; 3-A; 4-B.

European Invaders: Alex Tettey – Norway; Inigo Calderon – Spain; Tim Hoogland – Germany; Aron Gunnarsson – Iceland.

Derby Rivals: 1-B; 2-D; 3-C; 4-A.

Crazy Kit: Leeds.

Mega Wordsearch — Page 60

World Cup Special — Pages 64-65

Flashback: Ivan Rakitic.

5 Questions On Germany:
1. Thomas Muller; 2. Mario Gotze; 3. Joachim Low; 4. Per Mertesacker; 5. Algeria.

Camera Shy: Pablo Zabaleta, Martin Demichelis & Mesut Ozil.

Close-Up: 1. James Rodriguez; 2. Joel Campbell; 3. Tim Howard; 4. Daley Blind.

Spot The Ball: G15.

Brazil 2014 Stars: 1. Chile; 2. France; 3. Mexico; 4. Colombia.

Match Winner: Gonzalo Higuain.

Crazy Kit: USA.

Footy Mis-match — Page 72

1. The 'D' on Demichelis' shirt is missing; 2. One of the stars above Germany's badge on Gotze's shirt has gone; 3. Gotze's little finger is now extended; 4. The No.9 is missing off Gotze's shorts; 5. The Argentina badge on Romero's shorts has disappeared; 6. The ball has moved position; 7. The badge on Garay's sleeve has changed colour; 8. The stripe on Garay's left sock is missing; 9. A stripe has been added down the side of Muller's shirt; 10. The 'S' is missing off the advertising hoarding.

Five points for each correct answer!

MY SCORE /940

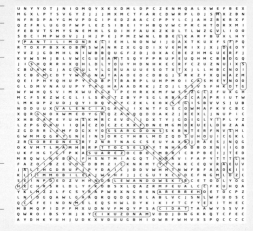

HOW DID YOU DO?

851-940	Champions League Legend!
601-850	Premier League Superstar!
351-600	Football League Wonderkid!
151-350	Non-League Veteran!
0-150	Own-Goal Specialist!

FREE! ISSUE OF MATCH FOR EVERY READER!